CD Included

T0040674

Get Off My Note, Get Out of My Way...
Please!

12 Original Piano Duets With CD

By
Anne Moot

Dedicated to the Music Forum for Piano Teachers of Western New York
with special thanks to Judith Burritt, my compass and my anchor on my voyages of
composition, and to Nida Semiavone for editorial assistance.
CD recorded by Robert Sawyrda, Local Publications.
Performed by Judith Burritt & Anne Moot.

Contents

CD Tracks 1, 2

PARALLELS

SECONDO

ANNE MOOT

108 - ♩

CD Tracks 1, 3

PARALLELS

PRIMO

ANNE MOOT

CD Tracks 4, 5

LUNA S GONE

SECONDO

ANNE MOOT

CD Tracks 4, 6

LUNA S GONE

PRIMO

ANNE MOOT

CD Tracks 7, 8

FLATS AHOY
SECONDO

I. SMALL WHITE CAPS

ANNE MOOT

136 - ♩

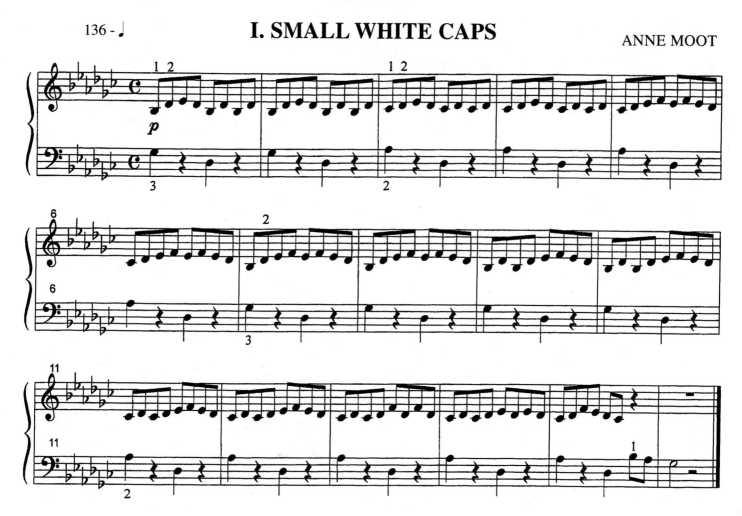

CD Tracks 10, 11

II. ROLLING SEA

112 - ♩

CD Tracks 7, 9

FLATS AHOY

PRIMO

I. SMALL WHITE CAPS

ANNE MOOT

136 - ♩

CD Tracks 10, 12

II. ROLLING SEA

112 - ♩

SECONDO

CD Tracks 13, 14

III. CALM

CD Tracks 16, 17

QUIRKY

SECONDO

ANNE MOOT

CD Tracks 16, 18

QUIRKY

PRIMO

ANNE MOOT

CD Tracks 19, 20

MELLOW

SECONDO

ANNE MOOT

CD Tracks 19, 21

MELLOW

PRIMO

ANNE MOOT

CD Tracks 22, 23

SPIFFY

SECONDO

ANNE MOOT

128 - ♩

CD Tracks 22, 24

SPIFFY

PRIMO

ANNE MOOT

CD Tracks 25, 26

GET OFF MY NOTE - GET OUT OF MY WAY

SECONDO

As fast as you can

ANNE MOOT

CD Tracks 25, 27

GET OFF MY NOTE - GET OUT OF MY WAY

PRIMO

ANNE MOOT

As fast as you can

CD Tracks 28, 29

LOOKING FOR SPAIN

SECONDO

ANNE MOOT

CD Tracks 28, 30

LOOKING FOR SPAIN

PRIMO

ANNE MOOT

SECONDO

PRIMO

CD Tracks 31, 32

LOOKING FOR INDIA

SECONDO

Humid

ANNE MOOT

CD Tracks 31, 33

LOOKING FOR INDIA

PRIMO

ANNE MOOT

2411

CD Tracks 34, 35

JAZZY
SECONDO

Swing It!

ANNE MOOT

2411

CD Tracks 34, 36

JAZZY

PRIMO

Swing It!

ANNE MOOT

CD Tracks 37, 38

SOUL

SECONDO

Largo   68 - ♩

ANNE MOOT

CD Tracks 37, 39

SOUL

PRIMO

ANNE MOOT

CD Tracks 40, 41

GLEE

SECONDO

168 - ♩

ANNE MOOT

CD Tracks 40, 42

GLEE

PRIMO

ANNE MOOT

SECONDO

PRIMO

NOTES... This is my first totally original work for piano four-hands, predicated on all the options of duet playing. The fingering and pedaling are subject to the needs and abilities of each player and may be altered, but the other details enhance the underlying conception of each work and should be observed. Use touches of rhythmic pedaling on Quirky and Spiffy. Since pedaling helps forge a link between duet partners, many facets of it have been explored throughout the collection. These pieces range in difficulty from easy to relatively advanced, - something for everyone.

PARALLELS........ An introduction to the problem of starting together. Players must anticipate the silence of each measure. To improvise start the Primo on E, the Secondo on C, a tenth apart. Try other parallel interval variations. The crossovers are optional.

LUNA'S GONE..... Introduce the pedal on each measure of this simple yet expressive piece for young and old. Feel the phrase lines, and shade the legato very subtly. Create a sense of longing.

FLATS AHOY.......I. Primo may be varied in rhythm (i.e. quarter, quarter, two eights, quarter: quarter, quarter, four eights: four eights, quarter, quarter). II. Practice the triplet patterns, isolated, to manage the continuity of the piece. III. Double the Primo two octaves above for a more challenged player. Then try Looking for Spain.

QUIRKY.........A Haydnesque technique. Players should be attentive to motivs shifting quickly from Primo to Secondo.

MELLOW.......A moderate waltz, with pedal on the third beat. Challenge of numerous accidentals in a rarely played key.

SPIFFY............ Find the clown.

GET OFF MY NOTE....... Speed challenge. Fingering is difficult but necessary to avoid collision. Secondo plays high above Primo. Develop a game plan for every physical movement. This piece is the essence of duet playing.

LOOKING FOR SPAIN...... Precision demanded in Primo playing hands exactly together. Secondo must dominate and be intense. Evocation of extremes in the Spanish idiom.

LOOKING FOR INDIA ...... Both parts explore an extended hand position that expands and contracts. Evocation of the exotic.

JAZZY...... Learn to bend the rhythm after playing it straight. Great introduction to chords in five-finger triad position.

SOUL......... September 11th could have been the inspiration for this dark minor key piece which finally emerges in the light of the major dominant. Focus on the sighing motiv, the Alberti bass and variation.

GLEE.......... Compare with Bach's convention of playing a triplet (Primo) against a dotted eighth and sixteenth (Secondo). Focus on the beginning of each beat, not the subdivisions.

Every duet requires a new approach to listening. You have to listen to each other to make it work. The usual focus on solo playing (mind, heart and body) is doubled. Both partners must prepare the tempo and learn to depend upon each other during performance. Love your partner and have fun.